Angel Double Letters

The Original and Complete Guide for the Meanings of Repeating Letters Shown By Guardian Angels

SONIKA TYAGI

Copyright © 2019 Sonika Tyagi

All rights reserved. No part of this book may be reproduced, stored or transmitted in any form or by any means, electronic, mechanical, phonographic, photocopying, recording, scanning, or otherwise without written permission from the author. It is illegal to copy this book, post it on a website, or distribute it by any other means without permission.

The intent of the author is only to offer information of a general nature. This book is sold with the understanding that the author is not engaged to render any type of psychological, legal, or any other kind of professional advice. Neither the author nor the publisher shall be liable for any physical, psychological, emotional, financial, or commercial damages, including, but not limited to, special, incidental, consequential or other damages. You are responsible for your own choices, actions, and results. No liability is assumed for losses or damages due to the information provided. In the event you use any of the information in this book, the author and publisher assume no responsibility for your actions.

Author's website: www.goldensunlife.com

ISBN: 978-0-578-56397-8

For God with LOVE and His LOVE,
For My Father Ved Prakash and His Guardianship,
For Krishna and Rama and their tremendous patience,
For the readers who embrace this Guide with pure intentions,
a desire for self-development, an open mind and heart.

CONTENTS

INTRODUCTION	8
THE STORY BEHIND THE BIRTH OF THIS GUIDE	9
SPECIAL QUESTIONS FOR ARCHANGEL RAPHAEL	

1. I SEE DOUBLE AND TRIPLE LETTERS AND ANGEL NUMBERS OFTEN, SOMETIMES EVEN 5 TIMES A DAY. HOW DO I KNOW WHEN I'M BEING GIVEN A SPECIFIC MESSAGE AND WHEN NOT? **11**
2. I WANT TO START RECEIVING MESSAGES THROUGH SIGHTINGS OF ANGEL DOUBLE LETTERS. HOW CAN I START TO SEE ANGEL DOUBLE LETTERS? **13**
3. WHY AM I RECEIVING FREQUENT SIGHTINGS ANYWAYS? AM I SPECIAL? **14**
4. WHERE WILL I SEE THESE ANGEL DOUBLE LETTERS AND HOW DO I BEST USE THESE SIGHTINGS? **14**
5. WHY DO GOD AND THE ANGELS USE THESE NUMBERS AND LETTERS FOR COMMUNICATION OF SPIRITUAL MESSAGES? WHY ARE LETTER COMBINATIONS SUCH AS "BU" AND LETTERS COMBINED WITH NUMBERS SUCH AS "A2" NOT PART OF THIS LANGUAGE OF COMMUNICATION USED BY THE DIVINE? **15**
6. IS THERE ANY RELATION TO NUMEROLOGY IN THIS LANGUAGE? **17**
7. WHY DO YOU OFTEN ADVISE THAT I REQUEST OR PRAY FOR THE ASSISTANCE OF THE DIVINE AND ARCHANGELS IN ORDER TO RECEIVE THEIR HELP? **17**
8. AFTER A RELATIONSHIP BREAKDOWN OR BREAKUP, WHY DO I SEE REPETITIVE VISUAL TRIGGERS, INCLUDING FIRST NAME AND LAST NAME INITIALS, THAT REMIND ME OF THE PERSON WHO I HAVE RELATIONSHIP PROBLEMS WITH? **18**

SPECIAL EMPHASES OF LETTERS PAIRED WITH 1	20
AA AND AAA	21
BB AND BBB	24
CC AND CCC	26
DD AND DDD	29
EE AND EEE	32

FF and FFF	34
GG and GGG	36
HH and HHH	38
II and III	40
JJ and JJJ	42
KK and KKK	45
LL and LLL	47
MM and MMM	49
NN and NNN	52
OO and OOO	55
PP and PPP	57
QQ and QQQ	60
RR and RRR	63
SS and SSS	66
TT and TTT	68
UU and UUU	71
VV and VVV	73
WW and WWW	75
XX and XXX	78
YY and YYY	81
ZZ and ZZZ	84
About the Author	88

INTRODUCTION

I begin this introduction with the sincerest gratitude and LOVE to the Everlasting Almighty God and Goddess, The Divine Father and The Divine Mother and Their Most Lovable, Deeply Cherished Helpers, The Archangels, all of whom have made this profoundly spiritual and healing Guide possible. I'm grateful to the all-encompassing Divine for providing me this transcription of a very special language that is being used by our Divine Helpers to guide and assist in the human experience. It is with LOVE that I provide this detailed and complete transcription of the Archangels' language of repeating English letters to you the reader. Once your curiosity embraces this Guide and the language it documents, you will start to receive sightings of Angel double letters. By referring to this Guide at each sighting, you will realize that indeed your Guardian Angels are conveying relevant Messages to you through your sightings.

* Consciousness in this Guide is defined as the totality of all conscious states of a conscious being.

LOVE,
Sonika Tyagi

The Story Behind the Birth of This Guide

Since about the age of 7, I had very frequent sightings of double and triple letters such as AA, BB, FF, ZZZ, CC1, etc. Intuitively I sensed something "odd" or "otherworldly" about these sightings that I couldn't put into words at a younger age. However, with no access to a spiritual guide nor a personal home computer and limited time permitted to me on school computers at this very young age, I quickly abandoned desires to know more about these paired letters. At the age of 15 after the death of special loved one, I started to have sightings of repeating numbers such as 99, 888, 1111, 444, etc. Having access to a personal computer by this age, I researched the meanings of the repeating numbers and letters I had seen. While I was able to track down the meanings of the numbers, I wasn't able to find any trustworthy and comprehensive literature on the repeating letters I was seeing. Furthermore, the meanings provided by numerological associations to the English letters I was seeing didn't resonate with my life experiences. Not having yet tapped into my ability to channel Ascended Masters and Divine Beings such as the Archangels for answers in my teens, I again abandoned my pursuit of the meanings of these Angel double letters.

Sometimes what is left behind has a funny and determined way of coming full circle as I would find out later in life. It's through my experiences as a psychic reader and medium that I would be pressed again with the pursuit of finding the meanings of the Angel double and triple repeating English letters I was seeing. Over the years of conducting psychic readings and mediumship sessions, many of my clients inquired about the meanings of the double and sometimes triple letters (BB, ZZ, TT, SSS, etc.) that they were seeing "all the time". Some clients saw them in street addresses and on vehicle license plates. Others saw specific ones such as PP and CC when they were exposed to negative influences. Many of these clients were also seeing repeating numbers (i.e., Angel numbers) such as 1111, 333, 999 and 22. Through me from their Spirit Guides, they wished to know whether or not their letter sightings also have spiritual significance. Though there is a large amount of information available online and in books about the meanings of Angels numbers, my clients indicated that they weren't able to find any resonating answers about why they kept seeing specific letters such as BB, ZZ, TT and HHH and why they felt intrigued by them. Their questions made me quickly realize that I personally was experiencing a very real and wide phenomenon of communication through repetitive letter codes for many years. I wasn't alone.

The answers they received through their personal psychic and spiritual readings with me provoked me to also start asking the Archangels about the meanings of the double letters I had personally become very accustomed to seeing over the years. Through the answers I received from Archangels and the large amount of questions I received from clients about this phenomenon, I observed that indeed specific letters take on specific meanings when they appear doubly or in triples. They form a spiritual communication language. Due to the lack of availability of credible information about this communication phenomenon that is experienced by many people around the world, I decided to download this entire language from the Archangels and transcribe it into this Guide by channeling Them.

My request for this complete language was answered by Archangel Raphael when I began my channeling. He served as a conduit for the composite Voice of all Archangels and Divine Beings in the development of this Guide. Thus, all Messages offered in this Guide have been provided through Archangel Raphael. In addition to collecting and transcribing the meanings of Angel double letters, I also took this opportunity to pose several interesting questions to Archangel Raphael (that readers would also likely ponder) to help readers further understand the phenomenon of God and the Archangels using codes such as repeating English alphabet letters, numbers and number sequences to communicate Their Guidance to us, the children of God.

SPECIAL QUESTIONS FOR ARCHANGEL RAPHAEL

Here are the additional questions I posed to Archangel Raphael on behalf of readers and His Answers:

1. I see double and triple letters and Angel numbers often, sometimes even 5 to 7 times a day. Are the Archangels communicating Messages to me every single time I see them? How do I know when I'm being given a specific Message and when not?

Archangel Raphael:

"Dear Children of God,

We are full of joy in providing you various tools through which you are able to hear from Us and gain security in the knowledge that your Guardian Angels love you and are with you. Trust wholeheartedly that when you are meant to become aware of a specific Message from Us you will be guided to that Message. It's important to not forcibly seek out and not seek out repeatedly Our special codes of communication, but let them willingly reach your eyes. We provide very or extremely frequent sightings of repeating letters and numbers for two meaningful purposes:

    1. We want to give you confirmation that We are closely watching over the developments of your life and your evolution. You are not alone and have Helpers in Us. We don't want you to feel alone. You are not separated from Us. By exposing you to very frequent sightings of our languages We are reiterating and instilling in your consciousness the knowledge that We are truly One with you.

    2. During the period in which you are exposed to these very frequent sightings, We want you to recognize that your spirit is undergoing a very pertinent transition. Thus Our wish for you is that you take your spiritual growth especially seriously during this period of frequent sightings and embrace beneficial spiritual

activities. For some children of God this period will last a couple of months or a few years, and for others it will last up to about three decades. There is a rapid period of spiritual advancement. It will involve the shedding of unhelpful karmas carried over from your past lives and even relationship separations or transformations. Your devotion to your spiritual evolution will be tested during this entire time period. You will be exposed to new spiritual knowledge. Lightworkers, spiritualists and other healers, who walk in Truth and have chosen to carry God's work on their shoulders with purity, will help Us serve you during this very important time. We will guide you further on your spirit's path toward heightened enlightenment and ultimate liberation. Thus, We encourage you to acknowledge increasing frequencies of your sightings of repeating letters and numbers. The increases are meaningful.

Acknowledgment of Our Messages that are encoded in these special letters and numbers will occur in your consciousness; you will always be guided to learn what you are meant to know. Trust. You will be spoken to by Us, your Caretakers. **How will you know in which sighting [out of a frequent number of them] We are explicitly communicating to you the <u>specific Messages that correspond to the repeating letter or number(s)</u> you see rather than the two reasons given above?** Upon catching sight of the repeating letters or numbers you will suddenly sense something special about your observation. You may feel a bit stumped or held in place and unable to pull your eyes away. Energetically, you will feel a connection, a pull and intrigue as soon as your eyes catch sight of the alphabetical or numerical code. You will feel someone, or even that the letters or numbers want to say something to you. Some children of God will feel that they want to get closer to the double or triple letters, approach them and talk to them. You will have a hunch or intuition guiding you to explore the code you have just observed, likely because you have been exposed to that same repeating letter or number sequence a few or several times before. You will be led by Us to discover the very specific Messages held in those specific letters or numbers just as you have been exposed to and guided to this beautiful Guide. Trust.

Our languages of communication with you are not meant to be delivered in a controlled fashion. A degree of unpredictability or spontaneity helps to support the creation of sudden intrigue and fascination in the human observer's consciousness. This intrigue helps the child of God to be receptive to the Messages held in Our languages."

2. I want to start receiving Messages through sightings of Angel double letters. How can I start to see Angel double letters?

Archangel Raphael:

"Dear Children of God,

It is very easy to seek Our Love, comfort, pride and healing. We will always give to the children of God who seek Us and from Us. We are LOVE and We LOVE you. Know that by simply choosing to explore and embrace this Guide you have opened up a part of your consciousness to receiving LOVE, comfort and healing instructions from your Guardian Angels through Our language of double letters. Your consciousness has now opened up another avenue for Us, your Guardian Angels to use to build a loving and communicative relationship with you that will last your entire lifetime. We will use this language to provide relevant and needed Messages to you. It is now important for you to be ready to understand what you sense energetically the first and next time your eyes catch sight of Angel double letters as soon as the observation occurs. You will know that We are communicating with you if you feel a pull, tug or intrigue to follow through and seek the meanings of the repetitive code. By your genuine and purely positive willingness to discover the Divine Knowledge held in this Guide you have automatically created a new channel of communication and inspiration with Divine Beings. Your consciousness is the other half of this energy equation. Just as an electric cord needs to plug into an active electric socket in order to create a real energy connection and produce a useful result, your pure intentions and curiosity toward this Guide have established a new energy connection with Us." [Indeed it is this very same principle of an open and willing consciousness that allows for the most fruitful and accurate psychic readings and mediumship experiences. Your energy manifests your reality. Individuals who approach spiritual experiences with genuine receptivity are significantly more likely to have a positively resonating connection with their Spirit Guides during those experiences than individuals who choose to be blocked or defensively skeptical in their nature toward spiritual and esoteric experiences. In other words, it truly takes two to tango!]

3. Why am I receiving frequent sightings anyways? Am I special?

Archangel Raphael:

"Dear Children of God,

You are indeed very special to Us, your Guardian Angels and your Creator, God. You are LOVED and your entire lifetime is watched over by your Divine Helpers. When your consciousness shows signs that it is willing to engage in even the slightest connection with the spiritual facets of Our universal or common reality, you will start to be shown Our languages of double letters and numbers. You will then be led to research the meanings of these codes. For many children of God these sightings will serve as starting points for the exploration of additional spiritual enlightenment sources. We wish to communicate with you and you are ready to receive Our Messages. You are being invited to establish a more intimate, loving and communicative relationship with your Divine Helpers."

4. Where will I see these Angel double letters and how do I best use these sightings?

Archangel Raphael:

"Dear Children of God,

We, your Guardian Angels and your Most Loving God want you to embrace Our kind, loving and caring suggestions, instructions and insights transcribed in this Guide. Your embrace will foster the most positively enlightening experiences in your path ahead. The experiences and thoughts occurring in your life and in your mind are reflected to you in Our double and triple letters at the time of your sightings. Messages relevant to the practical and mundane facets of the human experience all the way to the higher spiritual aspirations of conscious beings are provided to you in this all-encompassing Guide. It's important to also recognize that Angel double letters serve as placeholders for the Messages We want you to perceive. The Messages take precedence irrespective of the letter pair through which They are perceived. We ask you to stay focused on the Messages "behind" the Angel double letters you see. We ask you to hold these Divine Messages close to your Heart.

Dear Children of God, We will show you Our letters that are documented in this Guide wherever suitable and necessary for your eyes to catch sight of them and for your consciousness to make a special connection with them. You will find them on documents and special forms, on the back of pizza boxes, in online usernames, email IDs, street addresses, signs, banners, in special certificate or confirmation codes, passcodes, automotive license plates and a myriad of other locations. We encourage you to be attentive."

5. Why do God, the Ascended Masters and Archangels use these numbers and letters for the communication of spiritual Messages? Why are letter combinations such as "BU" and "FZ" and letters combined with numbers such as "2A", "A2" and "CC3" not part of this language of repeating letters used by the Divine?

Archangel Raphael:

"Dear Children of God,

You are greeted with the Highest and Most Loving LOVE by your Guardian Angels. Your inquiry is an excellent one. Repeating letters and number sequences are optimal as languages because they meet the necessary requirements for the facilitation of regular or daily connection and communication that We desire to maintain with you. Inherent in their use is the ability to be easily recognized by children of God without the problem of overabundance, which for example exists with the use of colors and letters attached to numbers. Colors for example are certainly used by many children of God to maintain a personal communicative relationship with their Divine Guides. However, they are not the ideal choice for a system with universal or common meanings because there is an overabundance of color that every child of God is exposed to on a daily basis. This overabundance does not allow for easy delineation between repetitive sightings of specific colors with Divine Messages "behind" them and sightings that are not Divinely guided. The probability for confusion is too high as is the case with numbers combined with English alphabet letters. An exception is present with Our use of the number 1, a number that holds profound spiritual significance that, when presented alongside English alphabet letters, helps the child of God become aware of Our Presence. [A section in this Guide is devoted to letters combined with the number 1.] Furthermore, confusion may arise as to what color is being observed by the human eye due to the fluid nature of colors. Though double and triple English alphabet letters and numbers are visually expressed and used everyday, their occurrence probability is not overly high. They are quite easy for Us to arrange into sightings for you. Thus they remain optimal placeholders for Us, your Guardian Angels to encode Messages into and form recognizable languages of communication out of.

Single-letter combinations are not used as part of a universal or common language of communication by your Divine Helpers due to their inherent overabundance. The same goes for English alphabet letters combined with all other numbers except the number 1. Please know that for many children of God repetitive sightings of specific letter combinations such as "BU" and "FZ" come to hold special and unique meanings. For example, they may remind the observer of the first and last name initials of a loved one or an ex romantic love partner. Repeated sightings of such combinations signal to the child of God that he or she is missing a person, this person is thinking about him or her, a need to make contact or a whole host of other messages. They may remind the observer of a university or college that is very meaningful to him or her. If and when you continue to enhance your relationship with your Divine Helpers your consciousness certainly will become attuned to forms of spiritual connection and communication with Them that are unique and special to you. Together with your Divine Guides you will develop a personal relationship that integrates some custom codes, signals and other tools to facilitate spiritual communication with Them."

6. Is there any relation to numerology in this language you have allowed me, Sonika to transcribe?

Archangel Raphael:

"Dear Child of God,

In this Guide you are presented with a Divine Angel language of communication and connection that is unique to Its Source. We have intentionally decided to use a letter and repeat it or pair it with itself to form an easily recognizable code. At other times We present the Angel double letters with the profoundly significant number 1. Our Messages "behind" the Angel double and triple letters you see are not based on any proposed numerical equivalents of the English alphabet letters. We encourage you to explore and be attentive to the resonance and Oneness you experience as you use the Messages in this Guide alongside your sightings of Angel double letters."

7. In the meanings found in this Guide, why do You often advise that I request or pray for the assistance of the Divine and Archangels in order to receive Their Help and Divine Guidance?

Archangel Raphael:

"Dear Children of God,

We are always easily available to you when you call upon Us. Due to the respectful limitations placed on how much We can help you and help change the course of your destiny by the Principle of Karma and Allowance of Free Will by God, it is of utmost importance that you, a child of God directly ask Us for Our Assistance. By doing so, your consciousness signals to Us that it is welcoming Us to enact Our Divine Will in your personal lifetime journey. We are then permitted to formulate and reformulate synchronous events that will bring you the help, relief and enlightenment you are seeking in your request.

Dear Children of God, there are a variety of ways to request Our assistance. We encourage you to directly whisper or speak Our Names with clean concentration, send your requests and intentions to Us with your heart chakra energy, and be positively open to receiving Our Help. You do not deserve to live in fear. We are here to help you. Throughout this Guide, you are encouraged to directly communicate with Us using prayer, mantra chanting, meditations and any other forms of purely positive devotional worship that are set forth by your personal spiritual and religious affiliations. We encourage you, through this loving Guide that presents Divine LOVE to you, to attune yourself to the Most Magnificent and Everlasting Source, God. Rest assured, your calls for help to the Divine and desire to have more of Our Presence integrated with your life will not go unheard."

8. After a relationship breakdown or breakup, why do I see repetitive visual triggers, including first name and last name initials, that remind me of the person who I have had or am having relationship problems with?
[Since I have Archangel Raphael's attention, I thought I would pose a special FAQ I receive in my clients' psychic readings about this unusual phenomenon that some readers of this Guide have also likely pondered.]

Archangel Raphael:

"Dear Children of God,

We ask you to take comfort in Our Unconditional LOVE for you and care for your well-being. You are LOVED and will always be LOVED. Dear Ones this phenomenon of visual reminders occurs because subconsciously you are "calling out for" the person who has "walked away" in some form in the problematic relationship. It also indicates imbalanced emotional energy being held in more than one of your chakras. Memories that have not yet been made peace with exist in your subconscious. The visual triggers are synchronous events fostered by Us, your Guardian Angels to remind you that a part of you still requires healing, forgiveness and karma resolution. You are being asked to seek resources to bring healing and understanding to your unfulfilled, bottled up or heavy emotions, which are drawing the visual triggers toward your consciousness. We encourage you to remain attentive to these visual triggers and the encouragement for your healing that is inherent in them. They encourage proper acceptance and closure. We want you to know that We watch over your entire journey and want to help you discover healing and understanding. Prayer to and meditation upon the Divine and your requests for healing and peace will not go unnoticed and unheard."

Special Emphases of Letters Paired with 1

Examples: AA1, A1, CCC1, DD1, Z1, etc.

When your eyes catch sight of the number "1" following single, double or triple English alphabet letters and you are energetically intrigued or pulled by your code sighting, please know that the Angels are placing a direct emphasis on the fact that They are very much attentive to what is going on in your life and **are a very real Presence in your life**. You are also being asked to more carefully and thoughtfully focus on the Messages signified by the letters you see. Your code sighting is a signal from the Angels that Your Divine Helpers are closely watching developments and most certainly guiding you with respect to what the letter in the code signifies. The Angels are also emphasizing that Their Messages(s) "behind the letter" need to be accepted. It's an opportune time to interact with your Guardian Angels and speak your thoughts to Them just as you would with God.

AA and AAA

*The Angels give bountiful Messages. When you see **AA**, two or more of these statements or themes will resonate with you, and are being communicated by your Guardian Angels to help you understand what you need to stay focused on. When you see **AAA**, challenges or events related to some or all of these themes will be especially prominent in your life. However, Divine Intervention is very strong and your Guardian Angels are ready to help you. You are advised to ask Them for Their assistance and increased Presence.*

Excelling. (You're a star!)

YOU matter. The focus within or with-out may be all about you. You are a central personality in this situation. You may be very focused on yourself at this time and there is nothing wrong with your decision to look inward or think about yourself first.

A transition higher is coming or being obtained at this time. Look forward to a step up a "ladder" in your life.

It's an opportune time to bring simplicity into your life. Making lists and decluttering will be helpful.

OM. Be one and confident.

Your individuality is important at this time. Don't be afraid to express yourself. Be proud of your personality, unique viewpoints and behavior.

You are full of energy waiting to be expended. We lovingly encourage you to use this energy wisely because it has a tremendous amount of potential to bring about powerful manifestations in your life.

One of the luckiest positions any person can find himself or herself in is the position of the giver. It's time for you to offer the world a special gift, talent or expertise. You are ready. Be grateful for the position you find yourself in and how far you've come.

Like the central line that connects the two ends in the letter A, We are a part of your supportive foundation in your life. We, your Guardian Angels are supporting and encouraging you to express your individuality. Go ahead, plant a new "seed of You". You have our utmost approval.

Books, literature and writing are focal points. They may teach you a way of life. You may use them to boost your reputation or career. You are encouraged to write. You have a gift for writing and/or illustrating.

There is more for you to explore and learn. We lovingly encourage you to be more forward-looking and free of fear. We will help you approach new horizons and beginnings.

Bringing joy to others will bring joy to the Self, your Self. Bring joy to others. Be generous and give. We lovingly encourage you to be generous in what and how you give. Charity at this time will not only create positive karmas in your life but also help to dissolve and/or resolve negative effects (negative karmas) of unfavorable actions undertaken in past lives.

Long term vision is important at this time. We advise you to keep long term prospects and consequences in mind.

BB AND BBB

*The Angels give bountiful Messages. When you see **BB**, two or more of these statements or themes will resonate with you, and are being communicated by your Guardian Angels to help you understand what you need to stay focused on. When you see **BBB**, challenges or events related to some or all of these themes will be especially prominent in your life. However, Divine Intervention is very strong and your Guardian Angels are ready to help you. You are advised to ask Them for Their assistance and increased Presence.*

Progress and positive circumstances are indicated in practical and material matters [such as career, money, real estate, inheritance, physical health, important appointments, etc]. Expect favorable developments.

Projects with heart to them will do well. We encourage you to ask yourself if your heart is truly in what you are trying to achieve or what you are hoping for. Does your desire require you to put more of your heart behind it? If yes, be courageous and infuse more Love and Light into your desire now to ensure a positive outcome in the future.

Unions and partnerships are meant to flourish down the road. Progress and positive outcomes have been or will be won by those willing to work and play well with another conscious being.

You will blend well with someone else in a working capacity, and can achieve wonderful and meaningful results together. Good compatibility is indicated in the current or potential partnership.

Your individuality will be respected and shine while you are collaborating with another person. Don't worry, you will not be suppressed or overlooked. Your individuality will optimally shine through and also be seen as a gift to the partnership by others involved. You are an effective partner.

Self-help and positive activities that involve other people or animals will serve you well. You may serve others, including those from a different generation than you, by choosing to constructively share your time with them. We smile upon you joyfully and appreciatively as you engage in such activities.

Do you miss the toys of your childhood years such as toy cars, dolls and other toys and books? Your Inner Child wants to play. Let it! Embrace playfulness in your life and feed your Inner Child.

CC and CCC

*The Angels give bountiful Messages. When you see **CC**, two or more of these statements or themes will resonate with you, and are being communicated by your Guardian Angels to help you understand what you need to stay focused on. When you see **CCC**, challenges or events related to some or all of these themes will be especially prominent in your life. However, Divine Intervention is very strong and your Guardian Angels are ready to help you. You are advised to ask Them for Their assistance and increased Presence.*

A challenge is showing itself to you and may seem unrelenting. However hard it may be to believe or grasp sometimes, please know that your life is progressing, and there are results being achieved despite what remains a key concern on your mind. We will help you live more in alignment with your life purpose.

Trickery. A tricky person or element is causing confusion or hesitation. Recognition is the first step toward resolution. We lovingly encourage you to do your best to pull the wool away from your eyes.

There is not a feeling of complete security, closure or peace and comfort in some part of your life. Something may feel incomplete, inconvenient or frustrating. However hard it may be to believe or grasp sometimes, please know that your life is progressing, and there are results being achieved despite what remains a key concern on your mind.

Juggle the good with the bad as effectively as you can for now. We will sort this out for you for your highest good. Believe We will do so wholeheartedly. Keep Faith. Faith is the first step to reconciling a seemingly "unfitting" element in your life.

In a situation there may be two or multiple individuals, including you who are cautious and choosing to behave or proceed with caution and hesitation. Thus, you are not alone in how you feel or what you are intuitively sensing about this situation. While We encourage you to keep in mind that fear should not overwhelm and be gripping, there is something about this situation or aspect of your life triggering a cautious approach in you or others involved. Know all is protected by God, the Divine Source. Listening to intuitive hunches and gut feelings is the right approach to take at this time.

Inner work especially as it pertains to healing an illness, including a physical one, will be useful to integrate with the recovery of a part of your body or life. *As within, so without.* Please be one with this knowledge and act on it to help yourself and save others.

There is a cause that is worth fighting for or worth your contribution. "It is worth it." Out of a challenge you can create an impactful opportunity. You have the "green signal" or "thumbs up" for you to move forward with it from your Guardian Angels.

We encourage you to seek friendships and other associations more aligned with who you are now and who you are becoming. Learning which associations are the best for you to embrace and keep in your life is one of the most essential processes of spiritual evolution in the human experience. We will continue to help you wisely discern between favorable and unfavorable relations for you.

Growth is or should be your primary focus at this time. Please focus on and give attention to how, what and why there needs to be growth somewhere in your life and also inside of you. We lovingly advise you to keep yourself from engaging in activities and with people who stagnate your life. Stagnation needs to be avoided at this time. Time is a precious gift that cannot be recovered once depleted.

Please know that with every challenge and closed door you face, you are being redirected into a more fitting and suitable choice and path for you. Not getting what you want is a signal for redirection and *revision*. We lovingly encourage you to not be disheartened.

DD AND DDD

*The Angels give bountiful Messages. When you see **DD**, two or more of these statements or themes will resonate with you, and are being communicated by your Guardian Angels to help you understand what you need to stay focused on. When you see **DDD**, challenges or events related to some or all of these themes will be especially prominent in your life. However, Divine Intervention is very strong and your Guardian Angels are ready to help you. You are advised to ask Them for Their assistance and increased Presence.*

We encourage you to seek calm and peaceful environments at this time. Stepping into a more natural surrounding, being near water or spending time in the park will help.

It's time to cool down a bit. Allow a "cooling off" in this situation before you choose to speak or act again.

An element of your life is winding down, closing down or "taking a break". Please don't fight and resist this slowdown or closure. Know that all is happening according to The Divine Plan for your life.

Seek and embrace peace and stability in this situation as it is most important to do so. A very good outcome or result will manifest through stable conditions.

You are allowing certain people to take too much of your energy and power away from you. (For some, these people include family, colleagues and friends.) They are interfering with your mental and emotional peace and the positive potential of your life and your relationships. Shelter yourself from negative influences by imagining a protective white or golden light surrounding you completely from head to toe. **You are the chosen one! You are the architect of your life.** It's time to pick yourself up and take back any control you have given to others that rightfully belongs to you. Energy healing, seeking guidance from an adviser and retraining your mind toward a more calm state of being will help. We will help you find the approach.

Ground yourself through meditation, yoga, devotional worship and prayer, listening to gentle music and other forms of self-care. You will then easily and quickly see that things will turn out well for your highest good in this challenging circumstance or period.

Efficiency is important in any pressing matter at this time. We encourage you to make things more efficient in some part of your life. Efficiency is medicine for what needs to be "healed" right now.

We will continue to watch over you as you move toward efficiency and more stability in some area(s) of your life. We are your "backup". We have your back and will pitch in when you need a little extra help.

Family and career matters are very much on your mind. Any troubling or worrisome situations in these practical areas of life will be sorted out. Don't worry. Please don't be overly nervous. Nervousness and worry will only make the situations seem bigger than you, and exacerbate any intensity in these matters. Please know you are important and matter when it comes to your involvement in these areas. Stay focused on family and professional matters. Don't give up.

Attention and alertness are powerful spirituality-enhancing qualities. Knowing the power of awareness and being more aware of all facets of a situation (sides to a story) in your life will open at least one doorway for you. You will be able to make the best that can be made out of a situation or heal it. We lovingly encourage you to be truly conscious.

EE AND EEE

*The Angels give bountiful Messages. When you see **EE**, two or more of these statements or themes will resonate with you, and are being communicated by your Guardian Angels to help you understand what you need to stay focused on. When you see **EEE**, challenges or events related to some or all of these themes will be especially prominent in your life. However, Divine Intervention is very strong and your Guardian Angels are ready to help you. You are advised to ask Them for Their assistance and increased Presence.*

You're on the move literally or metaphorically! There are motivational and inspirational factors present in your life. It's best to embrace and go with the flow of exciting energy at this time.

You may be feeling extra playful or are really ready to learn new things. You may even want to or already have your hands involved in various projects or activities. The Universe [God] is supporting your drive right now.

Education and applying your intelligence and rationality to various projects or circumstances, including painful ones, will lead to useful outcomes and even prosperity.

Sometimes your excitement or emotions are not able to be contained. You are moving a bit fast in some area(s) of your life, driven by a particular motive, gain or pure excitement. You have quite a full plate on your hands that you are "plowing" through. A situation may feel "heavy". We ask you not to worry. We will help you to carefully choose where your energy, time, money and efforts will be most wisely spent. We will make sure that more certainty underlies your choices going forward and your priority reorganization.

It's a good time to focus on, pursue and be grateful for small delights and simple pleasures. You may still be waiting for a bigger "fruit" or blessing. For the time being, we encourage you to enjoy what you have and what you can create for enjoyment. Bigger blessings will come in due time.

We encourage you to pay attention to what God is telling you through events that will occur around the New Moon and Full Moon dates.

FF and FFF

*The Angels give bountiful Messages. When you see **FF**, two or more of these statements or themes will resonate with you, and are being communicated by your Guardian Angels to help you understand what you need to stay focused on. When you see **FFF**, challenges or events related to some or all of these themes will be especially prominent in your life. However, Divine Intervention is very strong and your Guardian Angels are ready to help you. You are advised to ask Them for Their assistance and increased Presence.*

Romantic, sexual love and other matters of the heart are on your mind right now. Union of the self with another is a fundamental or central theme. It is using up both your mental and emotional energies. We recognize and know what is happening within you. We are aware of your thoughts about your current reality. Know you have support and friends in Us as you work through these matters of the heart.

Your Guardian Angels encourage you to embrace the potential for new beginnings and renewed offerings in love and romance.

Your thoughts are devoted deeply or excessively to romantic and other matters of the heart. Some of these matters may have to do with children, custody or other parental concerns. It is important for you to be aware of the kinds of thoughts you are having at this time as they are holding you back from progress and positivity.

Self-confidence concerns are prominent. You may or may not realize that they are cropping up within you. Recognition is the first step toward resolution. We will help you work through these concerns.

Pregnancy and childbearing matters are relevant to you or someone who is important to you. We encourage you to be there for this person in his or her time of need. If you are in need of clarity and help from the Universe [God], then know that We will help you find the right help and answers.

We will help you see your way through to a healthy truth in your emotional life that is important for you to know. We will provide you a sign from the Universe [God] and it will come from outside of you. This sign or event will resolve any confidence issues. Introspection will help at this time as well.

Healing pertaining to children may be necessary at this time. We recognize a situation needs to be sorted out. Healing almost always involves healing your own Inner Child, who deserves the nourishment you open yourself up to. Your Inner Child deserves a lighter, freer, kinder and loving Earth experience. Healing with children through activities such as volunteer work, babysitting and playing with toddlers will be instrumental in helping your energy to become more positive.

Calm approaches and behaviors are encouraged when you're around certain people or people in general, including children. Embrace and attune yourself to the calm that emanates from the sounds that are made when gentle waves are birthed in a beautiful ocean. Be one with calm ocean waves.

GG and GGG

*The Angels give bountiful Messages. When you see **GG**, two or more of these statements or themes will resonate with you, and are being communicated by your Guardian Angels to help you understand what you need to stay focused on. When you see **GGG**, challenges or events related to some or all of these themes will be especially prominent in your life. However, Divine Intervention is very strong and your Guardian Angels are ready to help you. You are advised to ask Them for Their assistance and increased Presence.*

There is a major or minor sense of crisis and confusion. Your thoughts and actions require centering to help progress this situation toward a positive resolution. Your Guardian Angels are with you.

Silence will help ease the intense and challenging vibes of your situation. We lovingly encourage you to handle your written and spoken words with care.

Solitude and time spent in self-care practices and rituals such as yoga, exercise and meditation will help you now. Even activities like dancing and singing will prove to be helpful.

Know that forgiveness is a form of giving Love, of sharing your Love and sharing Our Love with others in your life. The power of forgiveness is underrated. It is a most potent potion for clearing negative karmas or the effects of a troublesome past and for fostering truly long-lasting healing. We ask you to give and receive forgiveness and will help you.

You will find yourself to be more forgiving or more able to maintain a softer, gentler stance after a period of inner work and self-reflection. Practicing breathing exercises will be useful too.

We are LOVE and We give you LOVE completely at this time. Our LOVE is a wholesome one and meant for you. We are surrounding you with Our LOVE.

Love is important to you at this time. We recognize you are in need of Love. Follow your heart's desire to seek Love from healthy, clean, pure and playful sources at this time. Doing so will strengthen your energy output and take away some of the "thirst". Even the Love you will feel when admiring beautiful flowers counts and will make a positive difference in your energy state. Thus, we encourage you to recognize that LOVE is abundant around you and comes in many sweet and kind forms in your human experience.

Gratitude and counting your blessings will help ease nervousness and anxiety. It's easy to forget what we have when we are overwhelmed by thoughts and fears of what we are missing or might miss out on. Please be calm and practice gratitude to receive more in the future.

HH AND HHH

*The Angels give bountiful Messages. When you see **HH**, two or more of these statements or themes will resonate with you, and are being communicated by your Guardian Angels to help you understand what you need to stay focused on. When you see **HHH**, challenges or events related to some or all of these themes will be especially prominent in your life. However, Divine Intervention is very strong and your Guardian Angels are ready to help you. You are advised to ask Them for Their assistance and increased Presence.*

Travel, transportation, exploration, adventure, freedom or liberation are key to a certain part of your life. People from different backgrounds or those situated far away from you may also be relevant. We lovingly encourage you to not neglect the signs you have been receiving pertaining to these themes. They are important for your next venture or step forward in your life.

Please do not be afraid to reach out and communicate with those far away from you. We encourage you to interact with people who are of different backgrounds and ethnicities.

International or multicultural relations and involvements are blessed and require gratitude. They are important to a part of your life, irrespective of whether or not you recognize them to be vital at this time.

We encourage you to think broadly. Expand your intelligence. Keep an open mind. We advise you not to bottleneck your thinking and create self-limitations.

It's important to stay away from self-limiting ideas and thoughts at this time.

A grounded open mind will help you make leaps of progress ahead of others at this time, including spiritually. Spiritual advancement is on the cards.

Father figures and fatherhood, including God are central themes at this time. We advise you to explore these facets of your life. We lovingly encourage you to give attention to this Father figure or paternal matter. Freedom and appropriate levels of freedom are also relevant at this time.

Your intellect has tremendous Potential. Optimistically focus on the benefits that are derived when one works to strengthen one's own intelligence and mental capabilities. You don't want to miss this chance to power up your mind's reserve of intelligence, knowledge and wisdom!

Be a guide or teacher. You are a guide or teacher.

Strengthening your consciousness or Higher Consciousness through relevant activities is encouraged at this time. Take time to engage in spiritual and educational activities, including reading, that engage your Higher Consciousness and help you manifest an even higher form of your personal Higher Consciousness wisdom.

Honor the guidance of your inner voice. Enjoy the power of sound and vocals. Hear the music and what it is conveying to you. It will serve you well to listen at this time.

II AND III

*The Angels give bountiful Messages. When you see **II**, two or more of these statements or themes will resonate with you, and are being communicated by your Guardian Angels to help you understand what you need to stay focused on. When you see **III**, challenges or events related to some or all of these themes will be especially prominent in your life. However, Divine Intervention is very strong and your Guardian Angels are ready to help you. You are advised to ask Them for Their assistance and increased Presence.*

Unity, togetherness and a sense of belonging are relevant. We encourage you to not ignore desires and any inner callings for unity.

Blessings from the Universe! Blessings from God to you! We are happy to greet you! We are ONE with you. We watch you, care for you and LOVE you very much.

Inner unity matters as much as outer unity. We encourage you to work toward inner unification of any confusing or fragmented parts of yourself and any problematic feelings about your self-worth. You have Our Support in the form of intuitive guidance in this endeavor.

The ties that bind need to be strengthened. Know you have the power to strengthen them. Stronger smart efforts toward family and other partnership matters are needed. Your intuition has already communicated to you what needs to be worked on. We encourage you to undertake the consistent inner and outer work necessary in order to maintain strong relations in your life.

We will heal disunity. We will provide you a path toward a brighter well-being. We will show you the light at the end of the tunnel, a path out of discord and disunity in two or more areas of your life.

Equality and fairness are keys to resolving a situation. All parties must embrace the value of equilibrium. We encourage you to be persistent and patient in your desire for a balance. Please don't give up on desires for resolution, peace agreements and justice. Speaking and hearing "I'm sorry" is very much still possible. All hope is not lost. Remember that no situation is ever truly only about one person or conscious being.

Faith and practicing faith will help you in the struggle toward more fairness. Devotional activities will bear positive results and fruit.

See eye to eye with someone else. This partnership can be worked out. There is hope and Our help for you.

We encourage you to pay attention to sounds and music around you. They serve as additional carriers of Messages of assurance, Love and healing from Us about your current situations.

LOVE. Know you are loved. Know that you also deserve and are being prepared to receive even more Love. All is happening so that you become capable of and open to receiving an even better form of Love in the future.

We encourage you to make someone else's life a bit easier today. It will make your heart feel better. The joy that comes from giving cannot be surpassed by any other form of energy in this Universe.

JJ AND JJJ

*The Angels give bountiful Messages. When you see **JJ**, two or more of these statements or themes will resonate with you, and are being communicated by your Guardian Angels to help you understand what you need to stay focused on. When you see **JJJ**, challenges or events related to some or all of these themes will be especially prominent in your life. However, Divine Intervention is very strong and your Guardian Angels are ready to help you. You are advised to ask Them for Their assistance and increased Presence.*

You can and will be able to breathe easier in a situation. Feeling good, refreshed or revitalized is on the cards. We bring you a renewed sense of being in an area of your life. We encourage you to embrace any lighthearted, new and more centered beginning(s).

A burden is going to be put in the past or has already been. A new day has or is about to arrive. Your toils and troubles are reaching an end.

Stubbornness is blocking progress in an association. We encourage you to seek out tools and resources to dissolve obstinacy. Prayer, mediation and counseling will help a situation take a turn for the better.

Your relationship to your roots needs a reinvention. Someone "on the other side" of the connection may be missing you. Be open to exploring your connection and feelings about your past and your roots. We will then guide you.

Power! Fairness and balance are being reached. They are helping shape an important understanding and a more peaceful, kind, gentle and truly helpful effect in a circumstance. We encourage you to keep plugging away with your attempts for justice. You will not be defeated!

The Wheel of Fortune is turning and progress is here. Sometimes progress can mean that what was once sweet turns sour and what was once sour turns sweeter. Progress any which way is a part of the cycle of life. We encourage you to embrace this Universal Principle. Keep the faith in the knowledge that ultimately all will be resolved for the highest and healthiest good. Ultimately, all will be well.

Know there is a right and true judgment about to be made, or one has been made. All involved in this situation are deserving of what is to come or what has already been delivered.

Your prayers are answered or are going to be answered in the coming days. A decision has been made by Us and it will be delivered to you. Please wait, and look upon Us with sincere Love, devotion and faith in your hopes for a positive resolution for the highest good of all involved in this situation.

You are waiting on or looking forward to important letters, packages, delivery service and mail. You won't be denied key information. Trust is relevant.

Favoritism or being favored are features in your life. Savor the delights that come with knowing and being shown that you are supported.

Love requires an outsider's perspective and some breathing room. We lovingly encourage you to take a step back or distance yourself from matters of the heart. The time spent apart will bring understanding, patience and perspective. It will be wise to respect and understand the value of healthy boundaries and time spent apart in love and related matters of the heart. Remember, no situation is ever truly about only one person or conscious being.

KK and KKK

*The Angels give bountiful Messages. When you see **KK**, two or more of these statements or themes will resonate with you, and are being communicated by your Guardian Angels to help you understand what you need to stay focused on. When you see **KKK**, challenges or events related to some or all of these themes will be especially prominent in your life. However, Divine Intervention is very strong and your Guardian Angels are ready to help you. You are advised to ask Them for Their assistance and increased Presence.*

Siblings and other familiar faces such as pets, friends and other family are relevant right now. Who you have become accustomed to plays a theme or needs attention. Someone or some people need you or are carefully thinking about you.

We lovingly encourage you not to neglect your obligations to a familiar face or loved one despite how hard or trying it may be to be of service to others at this time. Be there for your friends and siblings.

Now is the time to be responsible and show reliability. Rise to the occasion. Show leadership and know you have Our very powerful Leadership with you. We will encourage leadership and courage in you. Be a leader because you are a leader. Being of service to others is one of the luckiest positions any conscious being can find himself or herself in.

We ask you to be brave.

Positive evolution toward new circumstances, creation and

emotional growth will occur rapidly if you pay attention to what family and housing matters and goals really require.

We will help you with the power of Our Swords and Shields granted to Us with Grace from beneficent God. In other words, We will help you choose the right words and actions. Please be brave.

Housing, home renovation and other residential or property matters may be on your mind. If not, now is an opportune time to explore residential property involvements, ownership or investment. You never know until you explore and try! Thus, be willing to learn. We will help you figure out what you need to do or accomplish in order to make your housing dreams come true.

Reworking the set up of your home, workplace or study environment using Feng Shui and other energy arrangement tools will improve your outlook. These tools will also positively influence your physical versatility in those environments and overall home and work life.

You can't have joy unless you give joy. There are many ways to give joy and create happiness such as organizing a birthday party or family reunion. Start spreading joy and then watch your abundant returns come in! We favor you in this approach.

The Sun has the ability to shift your energy in a positive direction. Embracing play time with water and the shining Sun is encouraged.

LL AND LLL

*The Angels give bountiful Messages. When you see **LL**, two or more of these statements or themes will resonate with you, and are being communicated by your Guardian Angels to help you understand what you need to stay focused on. When you see **LLL**, challenges or events related to some or all of these themes will be especially prominent in your life. However, Divine Intervention is very strong and your Guardian Angels are ready to help you. You are advised to ask Them for Their assistance and increased Presence.*

Divine Beings are with you. WE are a Presence in your life. Please do not doubt Our help and support. We encourage you not to escape and turn away from your responsibilities. Remain faithful to your responsibilities in a concerning or not so easy situation. Keep faith in Us. We have faith in you.

Self-help, spiritual and religious texts will prove to be useful. Religious and spiritual principles and beliefs will be quite helpful and supportive should you wish to discover and strengthen your knowledge in them.

A special Message is to be found through a spiritual source that you have been disconnected from for a while. We lovingly encourage you to reconnect with this source again, be it a book, a psychic, a spiritualist or preacher.

Education and a sharper awareness as to what is truly occurring in your life currently will help you tremendously. We encourage you to reflect on your situations a little more. They require evaluation, which will be healthy to undertake.

We lovingly encourage you to use your responsibilities to raise others up alongside yourself.

Knowledge of your inner Self and the state of your heart chakra or emotional well-being is handy at this time. Let your inner Light shine and enlighten you.

You realize or hear something you didn't know before. New knowledge is arriving. Knowledge that you might have overlooked is recognized and becomes more significant to you.

We are Givers of important Knowledge. We will instill positive thoughts, emotions and approaches in your energy state to awaken your consciousness to this Knowledge. We will provide you more insights about your situations that need additional evaluation.

Extending a genuinely open mind and attention outward from the Self, even to something or someone who may be specifically calling out to you or for you, is what is needed at this time in order for you to make progress in a part of your life. You will simultaneously be instrumental in creating progress in a circumstance. We encourage you to reach out, reach in and foster connection.

It's a good time to spend time in your community. Exploring your neighborhood and nearby neighborhoods will usher in some good lifelong lessons. We encourage local engagements in your life, especially involving spiritual centers, places of worship and spiritual dialogue.

MM AND MMM

*The Angels give bountiful Messages. When you see **MM**, two or more of these statements or themes will resonate with you, and are being communicated by your Guardian Angels to help you understand what you need to stay focused on. When you see **MMM**, challenges or events related to some or all of these themes will be especially prominent in your life. However, Divine Intervention is very strong and your Guardian Angels are ready to help you. You are advised to ask Them for Their assistance and increased Presence.*

It is time to relinquish and defeat fears. Know you have a safe place in the Sacred Source, God. Look to your fears head on, straight in the "eyes". Do not be afraid to do so for We are behind you and beside you enveloping you in our protective Shields.

We provide you safety.

This is a time to understand better what you fear and why you fear. We will provide you useful progress in your genuine undertaking to discover the answers.

Heart health and your heart chakra are deserving of attention and care. There are needs unfulfilled in your heart. Your heart is needing. Please be attentive, pray and stay rational as We help you on the journey to fulfilling what your heart requires.

Service to the sick and any personal health matters must not be forsaken and ignored. We will help manifest good health and recovery.

Charitable giving isn't possible with only money and possessions. You can start giving today through dedicated devotional prayers, sharing positive healing messages with others and bringing positive emotions to others through nonmaterial means. Many have done so and accomplished great things in this regard. Your time is now. You can begin today. LOVE.

Physical death or separation is but one step in the ever progressive journey that every conscious being's spirit and soul thirsts after. Please do not be disheartened by such experiences. They are important portals for new beginnings to set in and must be rationally, peacefully and spiritually understood. We are bringing you comfort and the "big picture" understanding.

Religious and spiritual study undertaken by you, such as reading famous spiritual texts, will foster stable and solid forms of real healing and support that you will definitely experience.

Prayers and dedication to God and Us, your Guardian Angels will lead to rapid developments and blessings from Us to you. Now is the time! **Relinquish your fears and your tears to Us.** You are encouraged to do so and patience will show you in due time that We dissolved your fears and tears. We will resolve what you cry about successfully and completely.

You will realize in due time that your fears are an illusion and weaker than YOU. The potential in you to be bigger than your fears is truly already more potent than your fears. We will help you realize you were stronger than your fears ALL ALONG.

You are lovingly advised to foster, build and maintain a safer and more sacred space or home for yourself and your loved ones. We will help you in this endeavor if your free will chooses to follow through with Our Guidance. You are loved and supported.

A better way to trust is inherently present in the situational or relationship dynamic in which trust is an issue. Please pay closer attention to certain signals already emanating from this challenging situation or relationship to determine whether or not and how you can safely build trust.

NN and NNN

*The Angels give bountiful Messages. When you see **NN**, two or more of these statements or themes will resonate with you, and are being communicated by your Guardian Angels to help you understand what you need to stay focused on. When you see **NNN**, challenges or events related to some or all of these themes will be especially prominent in your life. However, Divine Intervention is very strong and your Guardian Angels are ready to help you. You are advised to ask Them for Their assistance and increased Presence.*

We lovingly encourage you to be at peace for what you wish or expect. Your expectation and expectant nature or inner will are guided by Divine Timing.

Timing is a key factor in this situation. If you are patient then you shall persevere. Part of what will birth the outcome will be your perseverance.

Something owed to you will be given.

Divine Timing is a very real element of your experience as a human being and all will play out for your highest good in the future. We lovingly encourage you to trust Us a little more.

You will see your Highest Good, a consummate basket of a lot for you to be grateful for, manifest in your future. However, now is not the appropriate time for this manifestation. Please look to the future peacefully and patiently. Do not watch the clock expectantly. Instead look forward into the unknown confidently Dear One.

We encourage you to look forward and take a slower or measured approach in your actions.

Sometimes "inactivity" proves to be ironically more progressive and fruitful than "activity". We lovingly encourage you to apply modes of action and inaction appropriately to various areas of your life and will guide you.

Everything will be balanced. The situation will balance itself out. Karmas will be balanced.

Foolishness or irresponsibility with money and resources may be a problem in your life (or in the life of someone you care about). Healing these kinds of material imbalances requires you to put yourself to the task of making practical changes while also asking the Divine for His or Her Support as you make much needed changes. You will receive the Support you seek.

Silent meditation and breathing exercises will be useful for you at this time.

You may feel like you're walking in a maze or around in circles, possibly lost, when trying to figure out who or what is the right match for you in this situation or desire of yours. Sometimes it takes more time to find a "best fit" than you thought it would or should. Compatibility (or becoming compatible to what you want to receive) is a process. We are right here alongside you, helping you find your way out of the "maze" and reach your "best fit" option in this circumstance, area or chapter of your life. Please know that God has not forgotten about you and your wants and needs.

Sleep issues, lethargy or dizziness are telling you something about your bodily, emotional, mental and spiritual needs at this time. Please do not neglect sleep and sleep issues. We show concern for you. Thus, please know that We are aware of what you are experiencing. You are not alone in your struggle.

You are holding a belief that in your life thus far you have not accomplished something monumental or important. We strongly and lovingly encourage you to please banish this misguided notion from your consciousness because it is untrue. Your life is a special one and your spiritual growth in it is even more extraordinary. There is a lot to be proud of in even the most "ordinary", expected or "normalized" accomplishments such as raising children, graduating from schools, becoming more spiritually conscious, liberating yourself from unhealthy circumstances and being offered a new job or promotion. If you wish to accomplish more, please know that We will continue to support you in how you positively exercise your free will toward achieving even more proud moments.

It's important to declutter and let go of specific old objects that are reminders of a challenge of the past. It's a good time to also declutter internally. You are lovingly advised to shed historical emotions and outlooks that no longer serve you well. Doing so will "advance time" for you or open doors to refreshing and enlightening beginnings.

OO AND OOO

*The Angels give bountiful Messages. When you see **OO**, two or more of these statements or themes will resonate with you, and are being communicated by your Guardian Angels to help you understand what you need to stay focused on. When you see **OOO**, challenges or events related to some or all of these themes will be especially prominent in your life. However, Divine Intervention is very strong and your Guardian Angels are ready to help you. You are advised to ask Them for Their assistance and increased Presence.*

Express yourself. We lovingly encourage you to put yourself out there particularly through the use of your words and voice. Your efforts will bear fruit and We will help you find the right words, tone and style in your communication efforts.

You are encouraged to communicate your thoughts, opinions and other messages through artistic avenues. Confidently embrace the power of artistic expression Dear One.

We encourage you to feel secure in your communications because We are sending this security to you. Be assured you are indeed managing communications wisely in this situation.

Efforts to communicate more or better are needed. Seek to improve in this area and We will provide durable assistance in your improvement efforts.

You will find additional useful Divine Guidance and information communicated to you through Angel Oracle Cards, books on Angels and Archangels and Other Divine Powers. Please do not be afraid to open yourself up to them. They are rich sources of knowledge for empowering your life through and with Us.

Know that WE ARE on your side. We are with you and helping you. Please do your utmost best to uphold faith in this knowledge if it is faltering at times. We are here to help you.

Follow your heart. Seek the beneficial pleasures your heart desires and please don't give way to negativity. Embrace the power of a positive mindset or a mentality set in delight. It's important for you to keep your thoughts positive at this time and in the near future.

PP and PPP

*The Angels give bountiful Messages. When you see **PP**, two or more of these statements or themes will resonate with you, and are being communicated by your Guardian Angels to help you understand what you need to stay focused on. When you see **PPP**, challenges or events related to some or all of these themes will be especially prominent in your life. However, Divine Intervention is very strong and your Guardian Angels are ready to help you. You are advised to ask Them for Their assistance and increased Presence.*

Alert, alert, alert! Please ask for help. Now is the time to ask for help. Ring the alarm. We are standing ready to interfere on your behalf and to protect you through this situation. Request Our help and you will definitely see positive changes occur in this situation.

Father God is with you and involved in a deeply spiritual and loving partnership with you.

We lovingly encourage you to understand the value of and responsibility that comes with a relationship with a parent, guardian, authority figure or child at this time. A partnership is there and exists. The need to collaborate well and adequately exists.

Being a parent is challenging at this time. Being a "mother" or "father" to a person or group of people who you lead or look out for is proving to be a challenge. Comprehension and communication are the keys to resolution.

Obstacles seem to be cropping up more often than usual. They seem persistent. Look to a leader, seek help or expert advice, or research the wise words of a leader in the area you need help. Help will be given by Us and We will lead you to the right resource, guide, mentor or teacher for you.

You want something from someone who has the power and ability to provide it to you, but are feeling a sense of obstacle or difficulty in getting what you desire. There is a time and place for everything to occur Dear One. Timing is a key facet to this situation involving the giver, guide or parent.

We lovingly encourage you to increasingly view Us as your Guardians as well. Seek Guidance and Guardianship over your life across your lifetime from Us, your Guardian Angels. We care for you. Base your day to day thoughts in this idea that We genuinely care for you. You shall be led to develop your consciousness to an even more evolved level, a liberated consciousness.

Peace be with you. We bring you peace. Shanti, Shanti, Shanti. Peaceful energies and vibes will be felt by you or you may already be at peace.

Divine Timing is key to your experience and expectation(s). We lovingly encourage you to be at peace with this truth and knowledge. God's Plan is unfolding and God is protecting you. God is your Protector.

Hate, fear, anger, impatience, toil and burden all fall under the control of the Divine, God. Thus, with this knowledge firmly planted in your mind, please do not fall prey nor surrender to these troublesome emotions that are currently excessively common in the human experience. Know that you are powerful and have Soul and Spirit, God's Divine Energy within you. You are bigger and better than to allow yourself to engage in these negative emotions and experiences. We encourage you to ask Us for help in limiting your connection and engagement with these kinds of negative forces of the human experience.

This is the promise of God: Loving, flirtatious, friendly, positively intimate or kind experiences are arriving in your life. They are meant to heal a part of you. We smile to you.

We lovingly encourage you not to restrain yourself unreasonably in your pursuit of abundance and blessings. If you really want something, then go for it! We support your good cause.

We, the Divine are change agents. Believe in Us and Our Power to bring miraculous, magical and sweeping change into many lives simultaneously and graciously. Your belief will birth the seed for a more stable union between Us and you that will show Itself in highly positive experiences in your current lifetime.

QQ AND QQQ

*The Angels give bountiful Messages. When you see **QQ**, two or more of these statements or themes will resonate with you, and are being communicated by your Guardian Angels to help you understand what you need to stay focused on. When you see **QQQ**, challenges or events related to some or all of these themes will be especially prominent in your life. However, Divine Intervention is very strong and your Guardian Angels are ready to help you. You are advised to ask Them for Their assistance and increased Presence.*

We guide you to rest. Something needs to be given a rest. A break is needed. A wait and watch period is truly necessary in a situation.

Closure is being reached but the process may be tumultuous or laden with anger and other emotions. We encourage you to be aware of expressions of the opposite of rest such as anger and restlessness.

Choose rest or to back away. We lovingly encourage you to give way. It's ok to give up sometimes. This time "surrender" will be precisely what leads to a future success. Step back a bit and allow ease. Later on when you return you will make rapid or demonstrable progress and succeed.

You are at an important juncture in your journey. You have reached a pit stop or a crossroad. You are focusing too much on one side or perspective; there is a severe or striking sense of imbalance in some area of your life. We lovingly encourage you to understand why you are allowing yourself to feed this imbalance further. Reverse course or rest. We encourage you to reach "the middle ground".

If you feel now is not the time to rest, then moderation is the best next wise approach in your progress or process. Assessment will prove to be valuable.

If you feel now is not the time to physically rest, then moderation and increased deployment of mental energy are the best next wise approaches in your progress or process. Assessment will prove to be valuable.

Much work is to be done and still ahead of you. You have a purposeful and relevant future. A path is destined to surface ahead in your life for you to lay your bricks on. A specific path is part of your future. We encourage you to trust and believe that it is uniquely yours.

Doing something a bit edgy, taboo, risqué or risky may be on your mind. You might have already engaged in such an activity or association. Please be aware of the pros and cons of your engagement with this unusual or quirky element in your life. Some children of God will recognize that healing is necessary. We encourage you to pursue healing. We lovingly encourage you to be truly conscious of this engagement or association and all that is involved with it. Thinking carefully before acting will be beneficial.

Healing and wisdom can be found by you in Our Arms and Wings. Rest your anxieties and troubles in Us. Come to Us for spiritual help and practice. We stand ready to give help, useful advice and enlightenment to you. We will answer your prayers. Have faith and trust in Us.

Your efforts and prayers have been adequate. You have given this situation or desire all that was necessary of you or in your control. Allow Us, your Guardian Angels and God to take over now and help you manifest what you desire. We will enact experiences that will lead you to meet your goals. In due time you will receive your rewards and your prayers will bear fruit. Until then, We lovingly encourage you to continue practicing faith and to maintain the levels of inner and outer control that fall within your capabilities at this time in your life. Please know God's Gift is always perfect. Your rewards will come in the form of beginnings, closure, blessings and miracles.

RR AND RRR

*The Angels give bountiful Messages. When you see **RR**, two or more of these statements or themes will resonate with you, and are being communicated by your Guardian Angels to help you understand what you need to stay focused on. When you see **RRR**, challenges or events related to some or all of these themes will be especially prominent in your life. However, Divine Intervention is very strong and your Guardian Angels are ready to help you. You are advised to ask Them for Their assistance and increased Presence.*

Written or spoken words require reconfiguration and need to come into an appropriate balance.

Indecision often indicates that a key piece of information or wisdom is missing. Do your best to locate the knowledge you do not have yet about a confusing or troublesome situation. Once you become more aware you will be able to move forward and out of a rut. Knowledge truly is help and power!

We lovingly encourage you to be open to suggestions and help. You are resisting or are not completely open to new perspectives or a different line of thinking.

A "regal" attitude will not serve you best in this situation. You or someone may be resistant to communicate and in a more collaborative way. We lovingly encourage you to maintain a peaceful approach in this association and be responsive rather than resistant. Shifts in perspectives are needed in your situations.

Enlightenment will come. We will shed Light on something relevant in your life and within you.

We lovingly encourage you to be open to communication and collaboration. Accept differences. Resistance and control will only limit the expression of your Higher Self.

A step up "the ladder" is coming for you. Know it is truly yours; you are ready for it and it belongs to you. Confidently own it. More gifts are to be received.

Once you own up to a facet of your Self honestly and responsibly you will be freed. You will see new self-development and self-exploration opportunities gradually become abundant ahead of you.

We lovingly encourage you to seek mercy in order to bring forth progress. Choosing forgiveness and compassion over resistance is the smart choice at this time both as a parent or leader and as a child of God.

A surrogate, parental or authority figure desires and is trying to help you. This conscious being is merciful, sympathetic and empathetic.

A relationship with a sister, mother, cousin or other female family member needs attention. Help will reach you from a female family member. Be open to receiving this help and know that all will be worked out for your Highest Good.

The Divine Feminine within you is calling to you. Listen to the calling of the Feminine in you. You need to adjust how you are expressing yourself or "feminize" your approach in a situation. A more feminine, soft, compassionate and realistic approach is beneficial in some areas of your life now.

Gratitude.
Know that you will get ahead and have gotten to this point in your life with the help of others. We lovingly encourage you to show gratitude for the help you received from those who walked into the path of your life thus far.

Healing is key to a part of your life right now. It may even lead to prosperity and new beginnings. Your scope for healing yourself and/or others is wide. You may need to find healing at this time directly or indirectly through others. Please do not delay your healing pursuits. You will not falter in your healing pursuits.

SS AND SSS

*The Angels give bountiful Messages. When you see **SS**, two or more of these statements or themes will resonate with you, and are being communicated by your Guardian Angels to help you understand what you need to stay focused on. When you see **SSS**, challenges or events related to some or all of these themes will be especially prominent in your life. However, Divine Intervention is very strong and your Guardian Angels are ready to help you. You are advised to ask Them for Their assistance and increased Presence.*

We lovingly encourage you to shift carefully into a new phase, goal, house or endeavor.

You are speeding through some part of your life. You are missing what can be enjoyed more thoroughly or deeply. It's wise to slow down your speed and get to know yourself a bit more and a bit better before taking a leap forward or exiting a phase of your life.

A slow start is nothing to be embarrassed about or ashamed of.

You're deserving of a real treat that has arrived or will arrive in your life. You might have been expecting this treat. It may come in a form that is even better than you expected. Pleasure is to be experienced. We encourage you to savor the factor from which pleasure will be derived.

You are forgetting to stop and smell the flowers lining the path that you are rapidly traveling.

We lovingly advise you to show more discretion, care and discernment. Go back and review. Look over and think about something carefully with focus. It's a good time for reassessment.

Please don't push or speed up time too much. The timing or clock is in Our Hands. Be willing to positively embrace this truth and knowledge. It's wise to bow your head in reverence to the knowledge that you cannot control everything.

You are missing someone special to you. You may be unavailable to someone or toward an important activity. Now is the time to turn your attention to him, her or this activity.

Hope.
You haven't been able to devote attention to your spiritual self-care or religious activities. You may be missing Us, your Guardian Angels. Now is a good time to make efforts to reconnect with God and your spiritual or religious activities.

This situation is not hopeless. Please remain hopeful. We will help you see your way through to the Light, a new dawn.

In our cyclical Universe, our sorrows are eventually replaced with joys and our joys with sorrows. Fully embracing the knowledge that nothing lasts forever makes for an unperturbed and transcendental conscious being. We lovingly advise you to embrace the goal of birthing a more understanding and transcendental consciousness within yourself. It will help you tackle life's problems more easily and serve your life purpose well.

TT AND TTT

*The Angels give bountiful Messages. When you see **TT**, two or more of these statements or themes will resonate with you, and are being communicated by your Guardian Angels to help you understand what you need to stay focused on. When you see **TTT**, challenges or events related to some or all of these themes will be especially prominent in your life. However, Divine Intervention is very strong and your Guardian Angels are ready to help you. You are advised to ask Them for Their assistance and increased Presence.*

We lovingly advise you to find grounding. Anchor yourself. You may be getting ahead of yourself. Something requires more time.

Energy is scattered and there is confusion. You may even be obsessive or "possessed" by thoughts about a situation that involves struggle. We lovingly encourage you to embrace a grounded approach and perspective. Patience, a good tactic and a mindset of perseverance will help this situation enormously.

Smaller steps are best in this situation to obtain the best possible outcome. Be willing to take consistent and steady small steps to reach your goal. You may be experiencing stagnation, uncertainty or anxiety because you are focusing too much on what will ultimately be. We ask you to please shift your focus to what needs to be done next and away from the net outcome. Trust that when it is the proper time for you to receive the outcome, We will help you reach the best possible one. We lovingly encourage you to shift your focus to be one with the present moment and the present circumstances.

Love wisely, unconditionally and with conviction. When you will meet the lover you seek or the source for the kind of Love you seek, you won't be disappointed. We will Guide you. For some, We will also Guide you to help others find genuine sources for Love in their lives.

You are waiting too long for the perfect time and the perfect circumstances before you forge ahead with a plan, goal or decision. (For some, superstitions and related beliefs may be influencing your decision to not act.) Excuses may be cropping up within you or in other people, and binding you to unfavorable conditions. Please ask Us for help in sorting out fact from fiction and We will help you determine the right timing to act on a key matter before it's too late. You will be able to reach Us also through a credible spiritual adviser and healer such as the author of this Guide, Sonika.

Don't give up. We Love you and support you.

You can channel Messages from Us and communicate with Us through prayer as well. Be open to receiving important kind and special Messages from Us now and in the very near future.

Give things a little more time and effort or "muscle". We guarantee everything will work out. Your consciousness will also benefit as a result. Positive blessings from God are coming your way.

A well-planned schedule and a list of priorities will be helpful in this situation.

You will grow stronger and wiser. Wisdom is to be discovered by not giving up and surrendering in a situation. Please do not doubt, compromise yourself and sell out. Press on and be persistent. You will come out a winner.

A new sense of your SELF is forming. Who you are is being further refined at this time. You may not have even noticed yourself shedding off what no longer serves you well and "trying on something new". However, a change is happening within you. Know We are bringing this positive and useful transformation to you. You are being prepared for your future.

Swimming, rowing and other water exercises will help you work off a sweat or emotional state. We lovingly encourage you to pursue healthy activities to release pent up or confusing emotions. Healthy forms of emotional discharge or venting are advised at this time and in the short to medium term future.

Dance, fashion and other artistic pursuits that utilize physical body movement are favored at this time. Enrapture yourself.

UU and UUU

*The Angels give bountiful Messages. When you see **UU**, two or more of these statements or themes will resonate with you, and are being communicated by your Guardian Angels to help you understand what you need to stay focused on. When you see **UUU**, challenges or events related to some or all of these themes will be especially prominent in your life. However, Divine Intervention is very strong and your Guardian Angels are ready to help you. You are advised to ask Them for Their assistance and increased Presence.*

It's time to proudly pat yourself on your back and also thank others for helping you thus far.

As you raise your vibration, lifestyle or habits remember to raise others up and take them with you toward "greener pastures" and a more liberated Consciousness.

Grace. Gracious and cordial acts are highly favored. Someone is not as prepared and adept as you are in handling a task, situation or responsibility. You are encouraged to graciously cooperate with him, her or them.

You are an awesome and adequate parent, leader and guardian to another human being and/or to a pet. We encourage you to continue to be in charge or the leader of your "pack".

Know that you belong to a collective energy field full of other conscious beings. Every conscious being has his or her own stories, wants, needs, strengths and struggles. We encourage you to contribute your stories and energy in instrumental ways to this collective field. Join in a little more!

We lovingly encourage you to make the most of what you have. There is something about a situation, blessing or relationship that is not being fully explored, used for benefit or enjoyed. Something may be overlooked.

A home life or personal life balance is desired with various goals pressing for your time. We lovingly encourage you to place more focus on finding a balance between being you and pursuing what is most natural to you and also being part of a collective that needs your involvement as well.

It's a favorable time to share your time and money with a collective through volunteer work and other channels of giving. New knowledge will be rewarded to you for your efforts.

Taking a break and devoting time to introspection are strongly encouraged right now. We will help you find time for yourself and give time to others. We will help you strike a very good balance.

VV and VVV

*The Angels give bountiful Messages. When you see **VV**, two or more of these statements or themes will resonate with you, and are being communicated by your Guardian Angels to help you understand what you need to stay focused on. When you see **VVV**, challenges or events related to some or all of these themes will be especially prominent in your life. However, Divine Intervention is very strong and your Guardian Angels are ready to help you. You are advised to ask Them for Their assistance and increased Presence.*

You are joyfully proud! There is a blessing, proud achievement or victory to share. Now is the time to make it known to others.

You are feeling more secure and safe than you have in previous phases of your life. Rest assured that your present and future are secure.

Sexual energies are heightened. Sexual relations and feeling sexy may be on your mind. A person who triggers these sexy energies has or is about to arrive.

A very positive development is about to occur or has surfaced recently. Please embrace it and don't overlook it. We encourage you not to speed past it.

Someone is carrying you on their shoulders toward a zenith. Someone will hold your hand and show you "greener pastures".

Stress is abundant and some aspects of your life are worrisome.

You've stressed and stretched yourself quite far. Someone will guide you upward and onward out of troubled waters. Help is coming.

If you're thinking about a loved one or pet who has passed over, then know We have welcomed your loved one with Our open arms. Your loved one is safe and at peace, and you are not forgotten.

You inner world wants you to "shout" something in happiness, joy, worry or confidence to the world from a rooftop. We lovingly encourage you to express your pride, joys, sorrows or worries wisely. Then you will receive the correct or truly useful help, engagement or feedback from others that you need at this time. (For some, it's time to be ecstatic and feel blessed about something they have or are about to receive.)

Financial knowledge and security will come to you. Motivation and inspiration can be very powerful and effective healers for stuck or "contaminated" money energy in your life. We lovingly encourage you to find motivational resources to empower and charge up your ability to usher healthy money energy into your life. We will also be Guides to you in your quest.

WW AND WWW

*The Angels give bountiful Messages. When you see **WW**, two or more of these statements or themes will resonate with you, and are being communicated by your Guardian Angels to help you understand what you need to stay focused on. When you see **WWW**, challenges or events related to some or all of these themes will be especially prominent in your life. However, Divine Intervention is very strong and your Guardian Angels are ready to help you. You are advised to ask Them for Their assistance and increased Presence.*

Time pressures exist and time mismanagement is occurring. Time may feel a bit erratic and you have your hands full. We will help you cross off items on your to do list effectively and efficiently. Believe in Us and We will assist you.

It's in your best interest to learn from example. Avoiding mistakes is preferred over making them as you focus on how to best benefit yourself. Keep your eyes and ears open for experiences that will provide you meaningful lessons and knowledge. Don't be afraid to then put your newly-gained lessons into action.

We lovingly encourage you to remain focused on practical matters and duties. It's wise to be productive and practical for a brighter future and outcome.

Please accept help and leave some of your stress on Our shoulders.

Diversity enriches your consciousness and experiences. Gratitude for the diversity you are exposed to will enhance the benefits you're able to reap from it.

You are a change agent. Believe in your ability to be impactful.

Learning to delegate is important in order for you to make the best out of this situation and to reach an admirable result or level of productivity.

Wisdom and useful insights can be garnered by understanding and interacting with animals, such as farm and other work animals, and their lifestyles.

You will receive help from the most unexpected and surprising source. We encourage you to be gracious and welcoming of it. It will come. Help is coming to you.

You are full of energy and enthusiasm that can be used well and wisely for enhanced productivity. You will be proud of what your current hard work and efforts lead to in the future.

Environmental enrichment and care activities such as gardening and recycling are blessed. Flowers, trees and plant life are special to you. We encourage you to build a loving connection with nature, flowers and plants. Don't forget to smell the flowers and offer sunlight and water whenever you can, no matter where you are.

You have Our support and seal of approval for what you are working hard to obtain. We support you.

Wanting to be liked and accepted are on your mind sometimes. Know that you will do your best by being yourself. You will be influential and are respected. We encourage you to be careful about pursuing certain paths to popularity or influence. You will be at your best by being yourself, grounded and down-to-earth.

Who or what are you falling in love with at this time? Do you see a part of yourself reflected back to you in "the other"? We lovingly encourage you to more carefully examine who or what you are gravitating toward.

Food sources and consumption require a check at this time. Please review ingredients and their sources and health benefits. Your physical body matters as much as your emotions and mind or mental health. Food is a key focus right now and We will lovingly help you discover more about it.

Growing pains sometimes come with growing or evolving children or grandchildren. Growing pains sometimes manifest in our relationships with adults who are changing and evolving as well. Know that growth is a necessary process. We lovingly encourage you to pray to Us for help, support and Guidance on how to heal and dissolve stress and difficulty stemming from people in your life who are transforming.

XX and XXX

*The Angels give bountiful Messages. When you see **XX**, two or more of these statements or themes will resonate with you, and are being communicated by your Guardian Angels to help you understand what you need to stay focused on. When you see **XXX**, challenges or events related to some or all of these themes will be especially prominent in your life. However, Divine Intervention is very strong and your Guardian Angels are ready to help you. You are advised to ask Them for Their assistance and increased Presence.*

Sexual energies, expression or engagements are prominent. These experiences are providing you a teaching or lesson.

There is tension between what the heart needs and sexual needs. Varying needs are difficult to reconcile with each other and may not be fully served through one person. We encourage you to pray and ask for Our help. We will bring evolution in this matter and help you see your way out of this tense phase with Love and Light.

We are guiding you toward someone who fulfills both your heart needs and sexual needs. We will guide you to this more suitable person and out of any relationship or association that is best left behind. Prayer and spiritual and devotional activities are helpful at this time.

Secrecy. An affair or other activity is being conducted in secret. We, your Guardian Angels will reveal what, if anything, you are meant to know about this situation truly for your highest good.

A sense of mystery or a mysterious presence is captivating you. You are also encouraged to explore and learn about the esoteric, other life forms, mythology, astrology and other mysterious subjects.

We will help you in your exploration of knowledge that is truly useful for you to have. We will assist in educating and enlightening you.

In due time, through the course of your spirit's evolution you will come to know ALL. God does not wish to be hidden and is not hidden from you. This is an unbreakable Truth that cannot and will not be taken away from those who choose to walk the Path of seeking God.

Time has to feel right and be right for the Gifts inherent in these Special Letters that We provide you, as is the case in the most successful and blessed romantic couplings and marriages. In due time, at the right time you will be provided Special Blessings from Us, your Guardian Angels. Have Faith.

Sometimes when a part of your life feels suspended or unresponsive, it's wise to consider the circumstance to be a blessing. It allows you time to undertake important contemplative and reflection work about that part of your life and other facets of your life that also need your attention. We lovingly encourage you to give time to yourself and others outside of a part of your life that you may be or have been heavily obsessing, worrying or concerned about. Remember, other facets of your life need you too.

A mindset of perseverance is needed on the road to change. An understanding of how you can and will recover from any disappointments and "tough spots" along the way is also useful. It's time for you to make certain changes that you know about. We lovingly encourage you to embrace a flexible mindset in your journey toward change. Improvisation.

When you find yourself separated from and weary of the LOVE outside of you, you are encouraged to truly reawaken LOVE inside of you. It has always existed and will never be diminished. Please use the LOVE inside of you for self-care and healing. Share this LOVE with others.

YY AND YYY

*The Angels give bountiful Messages. When you see **YY**, two or more of these statements or themes will resonate with you, and are being communicated by your Guardian Angels to help you understand what you need to stay focused on. When you see **YYY**, challenges or events related to some or all of these themes will be especially prominent in your life. However, Divine Intervention is very strong and your Guardian Angels are ready to help you. You are advised to ask Them for Their assistance and increased Presence.*

A yearning. There is more to discover. Your Guardian Angels will help and protect you in your path toward a discovery.

We encourage you to protect your assets. Take count of your possessions and ask smart questions. Question more especially in a sales or bargaining situation or other practical matter.

Now is the time to make your words count. Make your speech effective. We lovingly encourage you to choose effective speech over trivial or wasteful chatter.

We provide you protection for your assets. We offer you help in a challenging situation in the areas of legal matters, money, business, finances, resources and belongings. We are watching over this situation and want to help you. We encourage you to pray and ask for Our help.

We lovingly encourage you to act with conviction and depth. Be confident in your convictions even if other people are not behaving or responding in the way you prefer. You will receive communication and connection.

Reaching out, networking and communication are useful at this time. We also ask you to question more, speak less and listen more.

There is still more to be learned and acknowledged about what is and what isn't. You will unravel more of the truth.

Intuitive intelligence will be handy as you try to figure out an association or circumstance for what it really is or what it really requires.

It's time to be serious, study and think through things carefully. We lovingly encourage you to be truly thoughtful, inquisitive and seek insightful knowledge at this time. It's time for your critical thinking to be exercised.

Reaching greater spiritual depth and acting on deep spiritual insights, rituals or practices are highly favored. Profound spiritual rituals and insights may not be so mysterious if you make the effort to dig deeper. You will realize they are not as hidden or mysterious as they are commonly and erroneously claimed to be.

Compromise will help you make the best out of this situation. In fact, compromise may be the best that you can get out of this situation. Know that at least this situation is not hopeless and something can be salvaged from it. Compromise will be helpful and healing here.

You or a loved one will be healed. Everything will be ok. There may be some ups and downs, but know that a safe and peaceful destiny is currently in the works by God.

Right now is an ideal time to do what is most comfortable and secure for you even if it means staying within the limits of your comfort zone or your budget. Trust that when the time is right and ripe, you will receive reassuring and definitive signals from Us that it is safe for you to step out of your comfort zone or what is familiar to you and do something different.

ZZ and ZZZ

*The Angels give bountiful Messages. When you see **ZZ**, two or more of these statements or themes will resonate with you, and are being communicated by your Guardian Angels to help you understand what you need to stay focused on. When you see **ZZZ**, challenges or events related to some or all of these themes will be especially prominent in your life. However, Divine Intervention is very strong and your Guardian Angels are ready to help you. You are advised to ask Them for Their assistance and increased Presence.*

A wake-up call is here or coming.

Celebration! You are overcome with zeal or joy. A favorable victory or achievement will be won.

Be your original self. We encourage the expression of your authentic, proud self.

We lovingly encourage you to loosen up and have fun. Please don't forget that life truly is short. Carpe diem!

We encourage you to take the next step you have been ruminating and carve your path forward. Your thoughts are on the right track.

It's time for beginnings. Remember endings are always followed by beginnings. This is a Universal Principle and Truth. You are coming into something new. A new dawn or a new prosperity is on the cards.

Resolution, peacemaking and keeping certain facets of your life as serene as possible are very important at this time. Be grateful for the lessons that are gained from an uncomfortable experience. Then, seek what can and will bring you mental clarity and support so that you can foster resolution. Resources for clarity and support include places of worship, God, counselors, spiritual advisers and other experts.

As you embark on the next leg of your spirit's evolution journey know that all has come into sync. Synchronous happenings include some beginnings for you. All is aligned and happening according to a special Divine Plan for your spirit.

You found THE ONE. Your Twin Flame is arriving or has arrived. You may be with him or her at this time. He or she is THE ONE! He or she is someone truly compatible with you. Your Twin Flame serves as an interesting reflection point and key figure for your spiritual evolution in your current lifetime.

Love and acceptance are important focus areas. Please be open to accepting Love. You may need to work on more kindly accepting the strengths and weaknesses in others now or in the near future. We will help you by giving you insights about how you can make progress with Love and acceptance.

We have welcomed all of your passed over loved ones with open arms and We are with them. We give Love to your deceased loved ones and pets and peace to you.

We, your Guardian Angels are with you. Please know We are your lifelong partners and with you at every step of your way forward.

New friends or distant relatives are highlighted. Smile! Happy or momentous occasions are expected.

It's beneficial to keep up with your to-do list now and even to try to pick up the pace at which you are completing or accomplishing tasks. Please stay focused on what you know must be completed. Engaging with motors and speed and racing activities are also favored. Encourage yourself a little more. We encourage you.

Thank you God.

ABOUT THE AUTHOR

Sonika Tyagi is an accomplished natural-born psychic, medium, Ascended Masters channeler, energy healer and spiritual educator. She confidently renounced her potential and path in the more traditional workforce to instead pursue work in the service of God shortly after graduating from Barnard College of Columbia University with a B.A. in Economics. She was also the valedictorian of her high school graduating class. Sonika is a self-taught Tarot reader, and publishes monthly video forecasts for the twelve zodiac signs using Tarot Cards and Angel Oracle Cards on her website www.goldensunlife.com. She has also produced a large and growing body of spiritual education on her website www.goldensunlife.com/blog that includes spiritual communications with Jesus Christ, Mother Mary, Shiva the Hindu God, The Buddha and culturally prominent figures such as the late artist Tupac Shakur. Her video content has earned her more than 3 million views to date and thousands of followers from across the world. Sonika actively provides personal readings that integrate predictions with motivational intuitive coaching to clients from around the world. Further explore and follow Sonika's work at www.goldensunlife.com.

Made in the USA
Middletown, DE
04 October 2020